W9-AGB-721

FOR KATHIE

sourcebooks

MARGARET PEOT

LET'S COLOR TOGETHER

A Shareable Coloring Book
for Parents and Kids

Copyright © 2016 by Margaret Peot
Cover and internal design © 2016 by Sourcebooks, Inc.
Cover design by Sourcebooks, Inc.
Cover images © Julia Nichols/Gettyimages, igor kisselev/Gettyimages

Sourcebooks and the colophon are registered trademarks of Sourcebooks, Inc.

All rights reserved.

Published by Sourcebooks, Inc.
P.O. Box 4410, Naperville, Illinois 60567-4410
(630) 961-3900
Fax: (630) 961-2168
www.sourcebooks.com

Printed and bound in China.
QL 10 9 8 7 6 5 4 3 2 1

INTRODUCTION

At the after-school program at Operation Exodus in upper Manhattan, I was going to be leading an inkblot workshop with a group of fourth graders, and was waiting for them to complete their homework so we could start dripping and splatting ink together. I was sitting with one little girl, "helping" her with her math homework. When she realized what a startlingly inadequate math tutor I was, and how little she needed me, she kindly let me off the hook by suggesting we color the dinosaur drawings on her math packet instead of doing fractions. She got us a selection of colored pencils, and we colored together, talking quietly, sharing pencils. The next half hour passed like time lifted out of the everyday, and both of us felt refreshed and connected.

Around the same time, I had become aware of the interest in and popularity of coloring books and coloring parties for adults. I designed some ornate coloring pages, printed out a few of each one on nice paper, and sent an email out to my chums asking what day would be best for us all to get together and color—envisioning tea and scones (or wine!) and conversation. Everyone loved the idea, and everyone asked if kids could come too. Of course! In planning our coloring party, we all realized that the kids wouldn't be content with coloring in their regular coloring books; they would want to color the same thing as the adults. The idea for this book was born out of planning for that coloring party.

On each spread in the book, there are two versions of one design. Sometimes one is more complex than another, sometimes a character or detail is selected from one design and enlarged on the accompanying page. That simpler design might be just the right complexity for a very young coloring companion, or you might swap back and forth with your partner, coloring each side as the whim takes you.

Thank you for picking up *Let's Color Together*! I hope it gives you and your chosen coloring partners hours of shared relaxation and enjoyment.

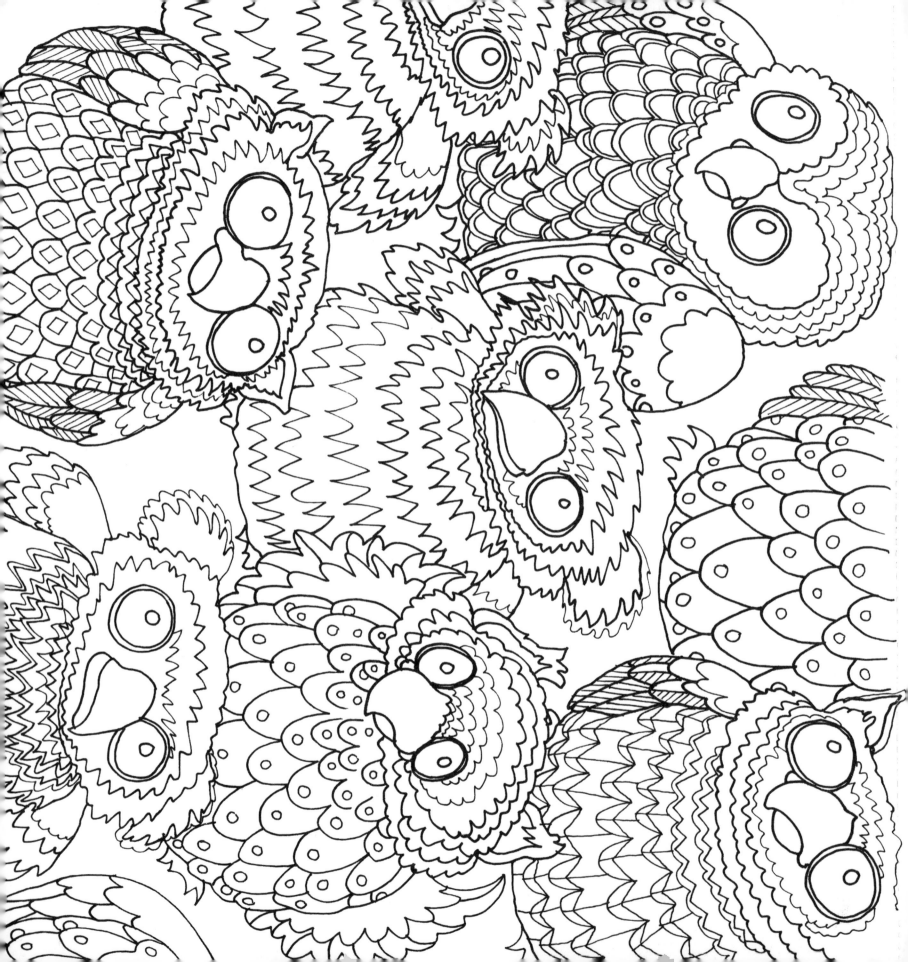

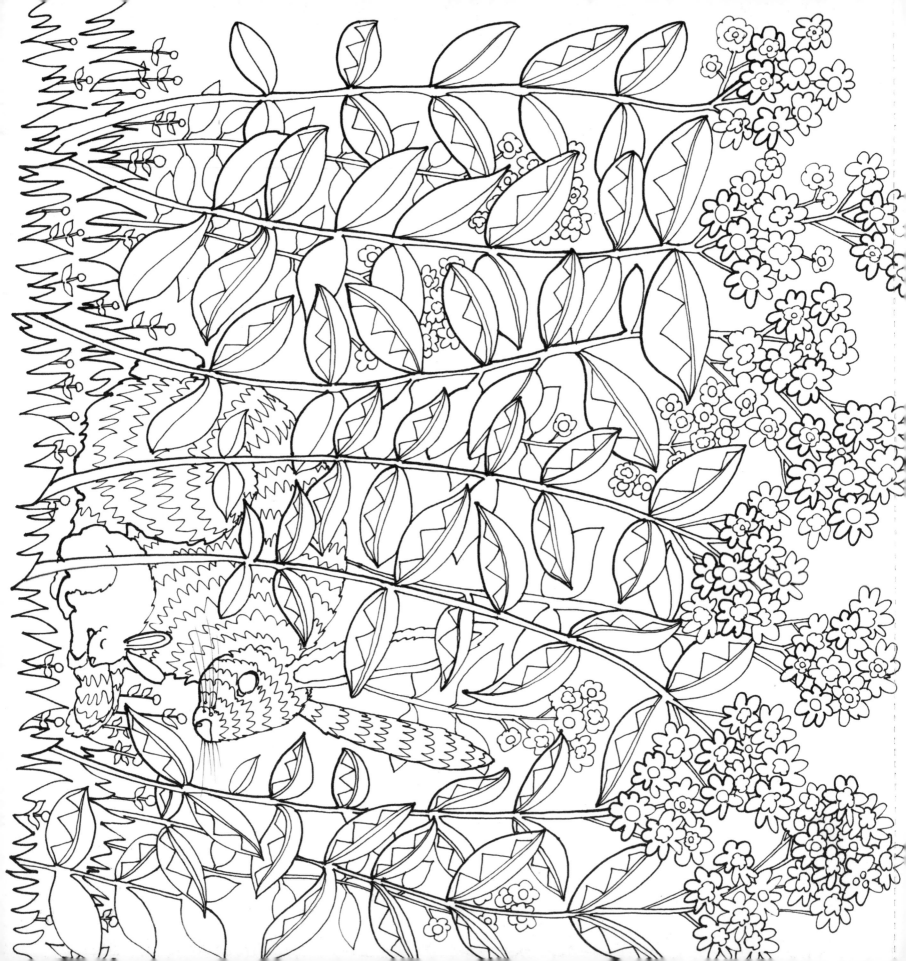

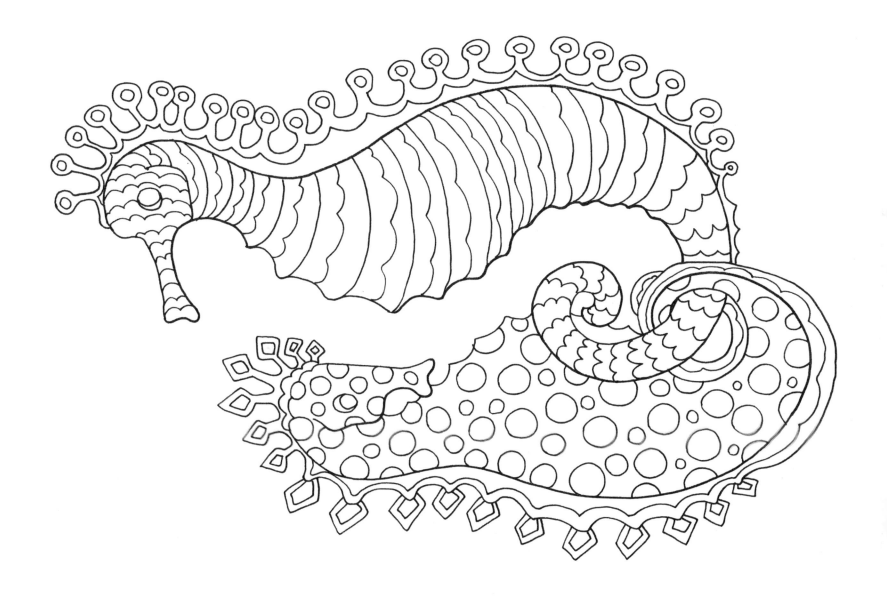

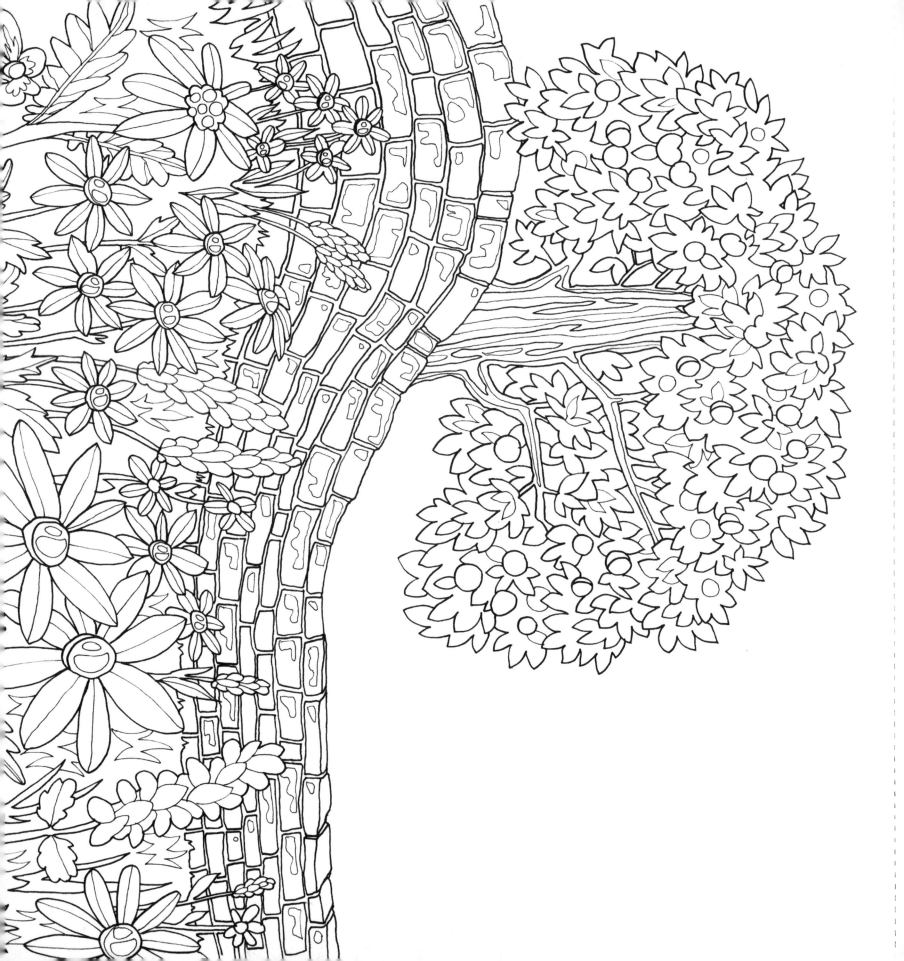

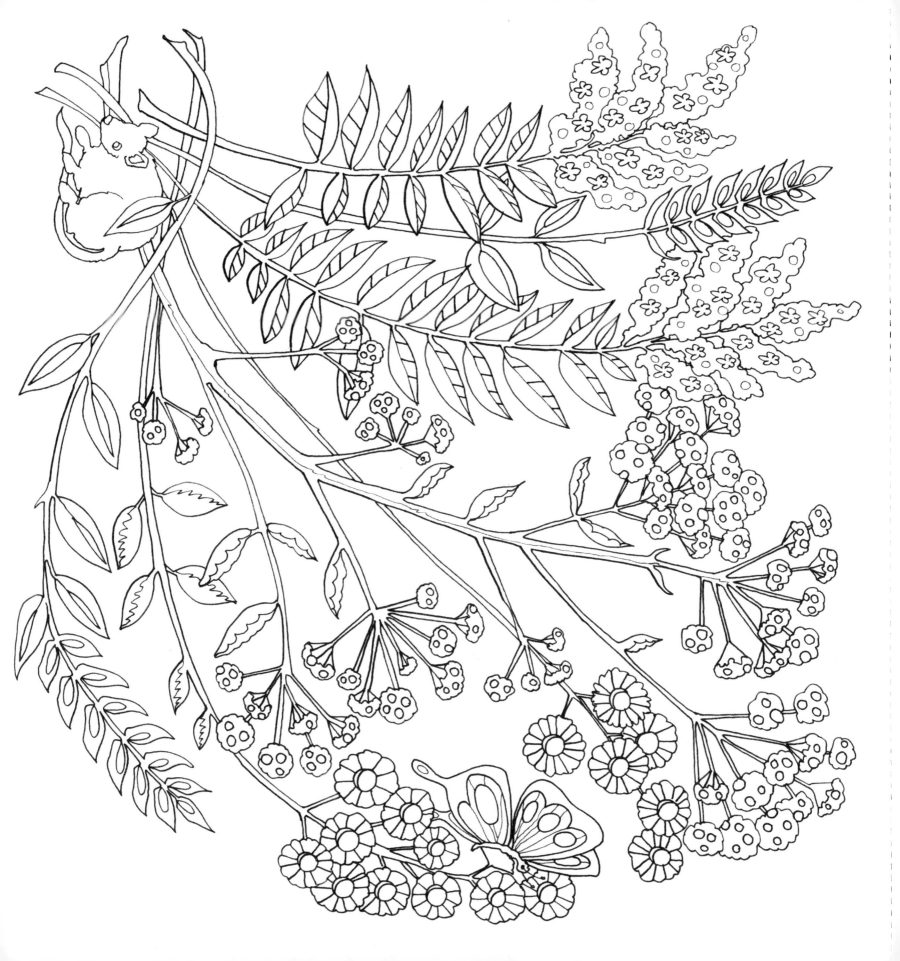

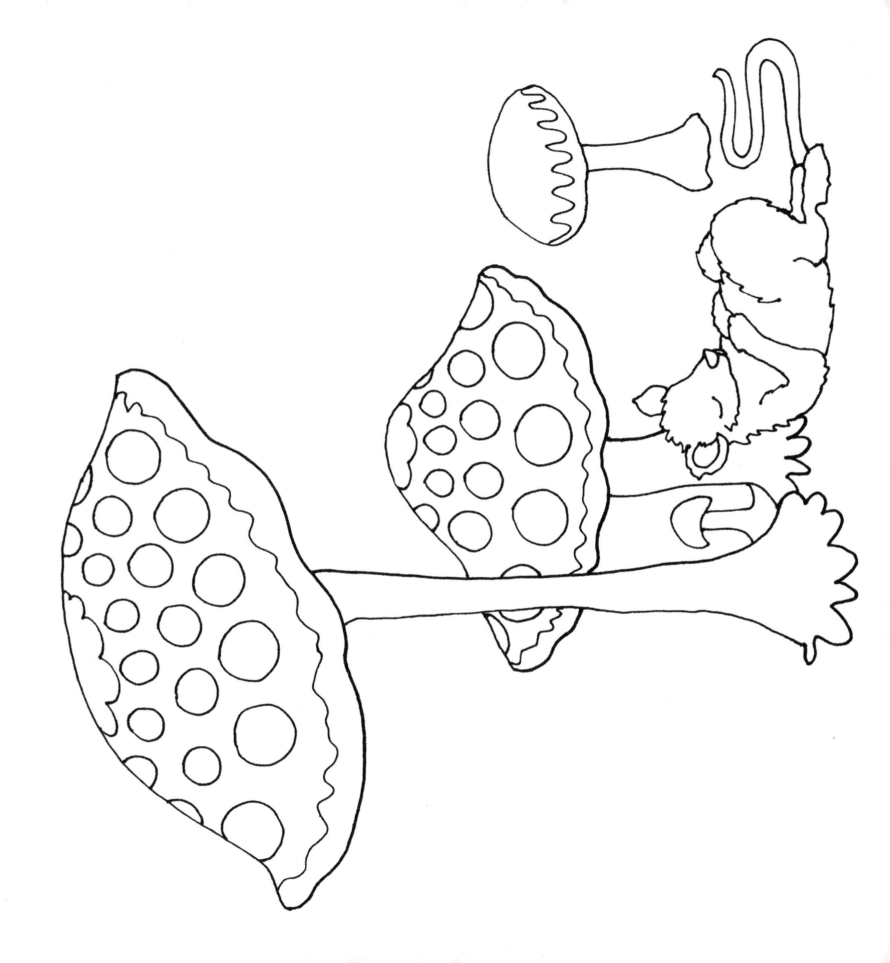

ABOUT THE AUTHOR

Photo by Peter Robertson

My mother said that when I was a child, I told her I was going to be an artist until I was forty, and then I was going to be a writer. I don't remember that exactly, but it is kind of what happened, with some overlapping—and I never stopped being an artist! I have written and illustrated several books, mostly about encouraging people to make things, including *Stencil Craft: Techniques for Fashion, Art and Home* (F+W); *Crow Made a Friend* (Holiday House), an early reader picture book; *Inkblot: Drip, Splat, and Squish Your Way to Creativity* (Boyds Mills Press); *The Successful Artist's Career Guide: Finding Your Way in the Business of Art* (F+W), and others.

The kinds of coloring books I loved as a little girl were those that included clothing. I loved to color outfits—not even draw them myself, but color the ones someone else had designed. Mom looked hard for outfit coloring books! Strangely, what I do for a living reflects that love of coloring outfits, as I paint costumes at Parsons-Meares, Ltd. for Broadway shows (including *Aladdin*, *The Lion King*, *Wicked*, *Spiderman: Turn Off the Dark*, *The Will Rogers Follies*, *Shrek the Musical*, *The Phantom of the Opera*, and *Mary Poppins*), as well as circuses, arena events, and ice shows.

I believe that art-making can and should be for everyone, so I present art workshops to elders, children, cancer survivors, writers, artists, and caregivers at The Creative Center's Creative Aging conferences, EngAGE Utah at the Huntsman Cancer Institute, Operation Exodus Inner City, and more.